T0162795

TREASURE CHEST

TREASURE CHEST

AUTHORIZED BY THE HOLY SPIRIT

PEARL COOK

WESTBOW
PRESS
A DIVISION OF THOMAS NELSON

Copyright © 2012 by Pearl Cook.

All rights reserved. No part of this book may be used or reproduced by any means, graphic, electronic, or mechanical, including photocopying, recording, taping or by any information storage retrieval system without the written permission of the publisher except in the case of brief quotations embodied in critical articles and reviews.

WestBow Press books may be ordered through booksellers or by contacting:

WestBow Press
A Division of Thomas Nelson
1663 Liberty Drive
Bloomington, IN 47403
www.westbowpress.com
1-(866) 928-1240

Because of the dynamic nature of the Internet, any web addresses or links contained in this book may have changed since publication and may no longer be valid. The views expressed in this work are solely those of the author and do not necessarily reflect the views of the publisher, and the publisher hereby disclaims any responsibility for them.

Any people depicted in stock imagery provided by Thinkstock are models, and such images are being used for illustrative purposes only.

Certain stock imagery © Thinkstock.

ISBN: 978-1-4497-3364-3 (sc)

Library of Congress Control Number: 2011962118

Printed in the United States of America

WestBow Press rev. date: 1/24/2012

CONTENTS

ABOUT THE WRITER

Pealene Cook was born in Hamilton, Georgia; and raised by her biological parents in Cataula and Columbus, Georgia. After high school graduation, she attended Albany State College, Columbus college, and Georgia State University. She majored in education. After accepting **CHRIST JESUS** as her Lord and Savior, she taught Bible classes in the Baptist Church religion for over twenty years. She taught children form preschool age into young adulthood. During which time, she also attended Bible college at Chapel Hill Harvester Bible College.

Pearlene Cook's major career efforts included over ten years at the Trust Company family. Currently, she is a retiree of the United States Postal Service family.

Most importantly, Pearlene Cook still has passionate heart for the **KINGDOM OF GOD IN JESUS CHRIST.**

THANK YOU ONE AND ALL FOR SUPPORTING THIS EFFORT.

FOREWORD

By

Pearlene Cook

A collection of the most exquisite, inspirational poems, song lyrics, essays, and short passages are compiled in this book. Various authors are acknowledged graciously throughout the publication: and to those unknown, much gratitude goes to each and every one of you. Let the word dwell in you richly in all wisdom; teaching and admonishing one another in psalms and hymns and spiritual songs singing with grace in your hearts to the LORD.

ACKNOWLEDGMENTS

All glory and honor and power and blessing and wisdom and thanksgiving and might goes to God Almighty forever and ever through our Lord and Savior Jesus Christ.

The author gratefully acknowledge all who have participated directly or indirectly in the bringing of this project to fruition, especially her parents, family, pastors, teachers, friends, and the many prayer warriors placed in her life.

PREFACE

To see a vision of the LORD is one matter; but to venture to express that vision in words, is a tremendous endeavor, indeed. That is exactly what is being hoped to accomplish in the lyrics of these poems, songs, essays, and passages written in this book.

When I think about the LORD pricking and filling my heart with His HOLY SPIRIT to inspire and admonish His people, it is too much for my finite mind to comprehend. Thank my GOD for knowing all about it and using such an insignificant person as myself. What a joy for someone like me, coming from the most humblest of beginnings, to feel the presence of the LORD and His very real LOVE. Oh, to be blessed to be a vessel for the LORD GOD ALMIGHTY, in any way, is truly magnificent.

May each thought, manifested in the book, encourage and bless you; from the youngest of His children to the oldest. Let's begin . . . .

CHAPTER ONE

MESSAGES, PASSAGES AND ESSAYS

OUR MOST AWESOME AND ETERNAL GOD

The LORD is in HIS holy temple, the LORD'S throne is in heaven: His eyes behold the children of men. For thus saith the high and lofty ONE that inhabiteth eternity, whose name is HOLY: I dwell in the high and holy place; also, with him that is of a contrite and humble spirit, to revive the spirit of the humble, and to revive the heart of the contrite ones. The mother of JESUS saith: For He that is mighty hath done to me great things: and HOLY is HIS name. Our GOD is quite mighty, almighty.

GOD saith: I am the LORD, and there is none else, there is no GOD besides ME, I the LORD, the first, and the last; I am HE, I am ALPHA and OMEGA, the beginning and the ending, saith the LORD, which is, and which was, and which is to come, the ALMIGHTY. Again HE says: I am ALPHA and OMEGA, the beginning and the end, the first and the last.

The earth is the LORD'S and the fullness thereof; the world, and they that dwell therein. For HE hath founded it upon the seas, and established it upon the floods (rivers). It is HE that sitteth upon the circle of the earth, and the inhabitants thereof are as grasshoppers; that stretcheth out the heavens as a curtain, and spreadeth them out as a tent to dwell in; Behold, the nations are as a drop of a bucket, and are counted as the small dust of the balance: Behold, He taketh up the isles as a very little thing.

The psalmist said: whither shall I go from thy SPIRIT? Or whither shall I flee from thy PRESENCE? If I ascend up into heaven, thou art there: if I make my bed in hell, behold, thou art there. If I take the wings of the morning, and dwell in the uttermost parts of the sea; even there shall they hand lead me, and thy right hand shall hold me. (Remember Jonah). One servant said: I know that thou canst do every thing, and that no thought can be withholden from thee.

Know therefore that the Lord thy God, he id God, the faithful God, which keepeth covenant and mercy with them that love him and keep his commandments to a thousand generations . . .

Deuteronomy 7:9

Hast thou not known? Hast thou not heard, that the everlasting GOD, the LORD, the CREATOR of the ends of the earth, fainteth not, neither is weary? There is no searching of HIS understanding. To whom then will ye liken GOD? Or what likeness will ye compare unto HIM? Again saith the HOLY ONE: To whom then will ye liken me, or shall I be equal? HE saith: Remember the former things of old (down through the years): for I AM GOD, and there is none else; I AM GOD, and there is none like ME. GOD says: Look unto ME, and be ye saved, all the ends of the earth: for I AM GOD, and there is none else. CHRIST saith: come unto ME. No man can come to ME, except the FATHER which hath sent me draw him: and I will raise him up at the last day. It is written in the prophets, And they shall be all taught of GOD. Every man therefore that hath heard, and hath learned of the FATHER, cometh unto me. (OUR SAVIOR, LORD)!

What a MOST AWESOME, ETERNAL GOD: OMNIPRESENT, OMNISCIENT, and OMNIPOTENT, BLESS YOU LORD GOD; such knowledge is too wonderful for us; thank you LORD GOD ALMIGHTY. Glory alleluia, indeed!

AKJV BIBLE
(Passages from throughout the books).

O Lord, thou art my God; I will exalt
Thee, I will praise thy name; for thou
Hast done wonderful things; thy
Counsels of old are faithfulness and
Truth.

Isaiah 25:1

BIBLICAL PRAYERS

AUTHORIZED KING JAMES VERSION

1. PRAYER FOR ALL THE CHILDREN OF GOD

These words spake Jesus, and lifted up his eyes to heaven, and said,
Father, the hour is come; glorify thy Son, that thy Son also may glorify thee:
As thou hast given him power over all flesh, that he should give
Eternal life to as many as thou hast given him.
And this is life eternal, that they might know thee the only true God,
And Jesus Christ, whom thou hast sent . . .
For I have given unto them the words which thou gavest me; and they
Have received them, and have known surely that I came out form thee, and
They have believed that thou didst send me.
I pray for them: I pray not for the world, but for them which thou hast
Given me; for they are thine.
And all mine are thine, and thine are mine; and I am glorified in
Them . . .
I pray not that thou shouldest take them out of the world, but that thou
Shouldest keep them from the evil . . .
Neither pray I for these alone, but for them also which shall believe
On me through their word;
That they all may be one; as thou, Father, art in me, and I in thee, that
They also may be one in us: that the world may believe that thou hast sent
Me . . .
Father, I will that they also, whom thou hast given me, be with me
Where I am; that they may behold my glory, which thou hast given me: for
Thou lovedst me before the foundation of the world.
O righteous Father, the world hath not known thee: but I have known

And all things, whatsoever ye shall
Ask in prayer, believing, ye shall
Receive.

Matthew 21:22

Thee, and these have known that thou hast sent me.
And I have declared unto them thy name, and will declare it: that the
Love wherewith thou has loved me may be in them, and I in them.
Amen. John 17.

II. MODEL PRAYER

After this manner therefore pray ye: Our Father which art in heaven,
Hallowed be thy name.
Thy kingdom come. Thy will be done in earth, as it is in heaven.
Give us this day our daily bread.
And forgive us our debts, as we forgive our debtors.
And lead us not into temptation, but deliver us from evil: For thine is
The kingdom, and the power, and the glory, for ever, Amen.
Matthew 6.

III. THANKSGIVING

Thine, O LORD, is the greatness, and the power, and the glory, and
The victory, and the majesty: for all that is in the heaven and in the earth is
Thine; thine is the kingdom, O LORD, and thou art exalted as head above
All.
Both riches and honour come of thee, and thou reignest over all; and
In thine hand is power and might; and in thine hand it is to make great, and
To give strength unto all.
Now therefore, our God, we thank thee, and praise thy glorious name.
1 Chronicles 29.

IV. DELIVERANCE

Be pleased, O LORD, to deliver me: O LORD, make haste to help
Me.
Let them be ashamed and confounded together that seek after my soul
To destroy it; let them be driven backward and put to shame that wish me
Evil.
Let them be desolate for a reward of their shame that say unto me,
Aha, aha.
Let all those that seek thee rejoice and be glad in thee: let such as love
Thy salvation say continually, The LORD be magnified.
But I am poor and needy; yet the LORD thinketh upon me: thou art

Then shall ye call upon me, and ye
Shall go and pray unto me, and I will
Hearken unto you.

Jeremiah 29:12

My help and my deliverer; make no tarrying, O my God.
Psalm 40.

V. ENEMIES

But thou, O LORD, art a shield for me; my glory, and the lifter up of
Mine head.
I cried unto the LORD with my voice, and he heard me out of His
Holy hill. Selah.
I will not be afraid of ten thousands of people that have set
Themselves against me round about.
Arise, O LORD; save me, O my God: for thou hast smitten all mine
Enemies upon the cheek bone; thou hast broken the teeth of the ungodly.
Salvation belonged unto the LORD: thy blessing is upon thy people.
Selah. (Amen).
Psalm 3.

VI. BLESSINGS

And Jabez called on the God of Israel, saying, Oh that thou wouldest
Bless me indeed, and enlarge my coast, and that thine hand might be with
Me, and that thou wouldest keep me from evil, that it may not grieve me!
And God granted him that which he requested.
1 Chronicles 4.

VII. TROUBLE

And now. Lord, behold their threatening: and grant unto thy servants,
That will all boldness they may speak thy word,
By stretching forth thine hand to heal; and that signs and wonders
May be done by the name of the holy child Jesus.

Acts 4.

VIII. PERSECUTION

Be merciful unto me, O God: for man would swallow me up; he
Fighting daily oppresseth me.
Mine enemies would daily swallow me up: for they be many that fight
Against me, O thou most High.

And it shall come to pass, that before
They call, I will answer; and while
They are yet speaking, I will hear.

Isaiah 65:24

What time I am afraid, I will trust in thee.
They gather themselves together, they hide themselves, they mark my
Steps, when they wait for my soul.
Be merciful unto me, O God, be merciful unto me: for my soul
Trusteth in thee: yea, in the shadow of thy wings will I make my refuge,
until
These calamities be overpast.
My heart is fixed, O God, my heart is fixed: I will sing and give
Praise.
Be thou exalted, O God, above the heavens: let thy glory be above all
The earth.

Psalm 56, 57.

IX. CONFESSION

And I prayed unto the LORD my God, and my confession, and said,
O Lord, the great and dreadful (awesome) God, keeping the covenant and
Mercy to them that love him, and to them that keep his commandments;
We have sinned, and have committed iniquity, and have done
Wickedly, and have rebelled, even by departing from thy precepts and from
Thy judgments . . .
To the LORD our God belong mercies and forgivenesses, though we
Have rebelled against him; . . .
O Lord, hear: O Lord, forgive; O Lord, hearken and do: defer not, for
Thine own sake, O my God: for thy city and thy people are called by thy
Name.

. . . Have mercy on us, O Lord, thou son of David.

Daniel 9; Matthew 20.

X. PARDON

Remember, O Lord, thy tender mercies and thy lovingkindnesses; for
They have been ever of old.
Remember not the sins of my youth, nor my transgressions: according
To thy mercy remember thou me for thy goodness sake, O LORD.

. . . God be merciful to me a sinner.

Psalm 25; Luke 18.

Thou shalt make thy prayer unto him,
And he shall hear thee . . .

Job 22:27

XI. <u>PRAISE</u>

Thou, even thou, art LORD alone; thou hast made heaven, the heaven
Of heavens, with all their host, the earth, and all things that are therein, and
Thou preservest them all; and the host of heaven worshippeth thee.

Who is a God like unto thee, that pardoned iniquity, and passeth by
The transgression . . .

Nehemiah 9; Micah 7.

XII. <u>SUPPLIVATION (SPECIFICS) PRAYERS</u>

A. <u>Watch in absence</u>—The LORD watch between me and thee, when we
    are absent one from another. Gen. 39.
B. <u>Discernment</u>—Give the king thy judgments, O God, and thy righteousness
    unto the king's son. He shall judge thy people with righteousness, and thy
    poor with Judgment. Ps. 72.
C. <u>Boldness with Healing Power</u>—And now, Lord, behold their threatening;
    and grant unto thy servants, that with all boldness they may speak thy
    word, By stretching forth thine hand to heal; and that signs and wonders
    May be done by the name of the holy child Jesus. Acts 4.
D. <u>To Grow</u>—Teach me. O LORD, the way of thy statues; and I shall keep
    it unto the end. Give me understanding, and I shall keep thy law; yea, I
    shall observe it with my whole heart.
    Make me to go in the path of thy commandments; for there in do I delight.
    Incline my heart unto thy testimonies, and not to covetousness. Turn away
    mine eyes from beholding vanity; and quicken thou me in Thy way.
    Stablish thy word unto thy servant, who is devoted to thy fear.
    Turn away my reproach which I fear: for thy judgments are good.
    Behold, I have longed after thy precepts: quicken me in thy
    Righteousness. Ps. 119.

If ye abide in me, and my words abide
In you, ye shall ask what ye will, and
It shall be done unto you.

John 15:7

E. Peace—Lord, now lettest thou thy servant depart in peace, according to thy word:

For mine eyes have seen thy salvation,

Which thou hast prepared before the face of all people;

A light to lighten the Gentiles, and the glory of thy people Israel. Lk. 2.

F. Controlling the Tongue—Set a watch, O LORD, before my mouth; keep the door of my lips. Ps. 141.

G. Word Power—Let the words of my mouth, and the meditation of my heart, be acceptable in thy sight, O LORD, my strength, and my redeemer. Ps. 19.

H. Clean Heart—Create in me a clean heart, O God; and renew a right spirit within me. Ps. 51.

I. Waiting on an Answer—Now, my God, let, I beseech thee, thine eyes be open, and let thine ears be attent unto the prayer that is made in this place.

Lord, hear my voice: let thine ears be attentive to the voice of my supplications.

If thou, LORD, shouldest mark iniquities, O LORD, who shall stand?

But there is forgiveness with thee, that thou mayest be feared.

I wait for the LORD, my soul doth wait, and in his word do I hope.

II Chr. 6; Ps. 130.

J. Aging—Now also when I am old and greyheaded, O God, forsake me not; until I have shewed thy strength unto this generation, and thy power to everyone that is to come. Ps. 71.

K. For Others—Give ear to my words, O LORD, consider my meditation. Hearken unto the voice of my cry, my King, and my God: for unto Thee will I pray . . . .

Let all those that put their trust in thee rejoice: let them ever shout for joy, because thou defendest them: let them also that love thy name be joyful in thee.

But thou, when thou prayest, enter
Into thy closet, and when thou hast
Shut thy door, pray to the Father
Which is in secret; and thy Father
Which seeth in secret shall reward thee
Openly.

Matthew 6:6

For thou, LORD, wilt bless the righteous; with favour wilt thou compass him as with a shield. Ps. 5.

L. <u>Love</u>—O righteous Father, the world hath not known thee: but I have known thee, and these have known that thou hast sent me.
And I have declared unto them thy name, and will declare it: that the love wherewith thou hast loved me may be in them, and I in them. Jn. 17.

M. <u>For Mercy; Not Punishment</u>—We beseech thee, O LORD, let us not perish for this man's life, and lay not upon us innocent blood: for thou, O LORD, hast done as it pleased thee. Jonah 1.

These prayers, and many more, are written for our strengthening and growth in the LORD.

By Pearl Cook

Call unto me, and I will answer thee,
And shew thee great and mighty
Things, which thou knowest not.

Jeremiah 33:3

OUR MOST PRECIOUS HOLY SPIRIT

The Third Person of the Godhead Trinity, God the Holy Spirit.

Although you are Alpha and Omega, we first read of your being in Genesis, Chapter one and the second verse.
And the earth was without form, and void; and darkness was upon the face of the deep. And the Spirit of God moved upon the face of the waters.

What honor can we possibly render to you for all you've done in our lives? Because of the coming of Christ Jesus, you ever abide with us. That is so Awesome.

Throughout the Bible you make yourself known by word and through symbols. Symbols used in the old testament section of the Bible; symbols used in the new testament section of the Word: pillar of a cloud, pillar of fire, breath, wind, dove, oil, fire, water, as well as light.

Your precious, amazing attributes can only be completely understood when we receive our immortal minds. You have personality, a mind, wisdom, and love. Let's back this up with scripture.

Personality:
For by one Spirit are we all baptized into one body, whether we be Jews or Gentiles, whether we be bond or free; and have been all made to drink into One Spirit. (The Spirit of unity.)
Quench not the Spirit. (Can be resisted.)
Grieve not the Holy Spirit of God, whereby ye are sealed unto the day of redemption. (Can be grieved.)
Now therefore be content (be pleased to) look upon me; for it is evident unto you if I lie. (Can be lied to.)
And whosoever shall speak a word against the Son of man, it shall be

And I will put my Spirit within you,
And cause you to walk in my statues,
And ye shall keep my judgments, and
Do them.

Ezekiel 36:27

forgiven him: but unto him that blasphemeth against the Holy Ghost it shall not be forgiven. (Can be angered; you really do not want to do that!)

Mind:
He that searcheth the hearts knoweth what is the mind of the Spirit, because He maketh intercession for the saints according to the will of God. The grace of the Lord Jesus Christ, and the love of God, and the communion of the Holy Ghost (Spirit), be with you all. Amen. (A mind to communicate With us.)

Wisdom:
God hath revealed them unto us by His Spirit: for the Spirit searcheth all things, yea, the deep things of God. (Spirit in us.)

Love:
. . . The Love of God is shed abroad in our hearts by the Holy Ghost which is given unto us. (The Spirit's attribute of love.)
Now I beseech you, brethren, for the Lord Jesus Christ's sake, and for the Love of the Spirit, (Returning love.) that ye strive together . . . .

Let's just list some of the characters you, Holy Spirit, bestow unto us.

Holy Spirit as our Leader
He took not away the pillar of the cloud by day, nor the pillar of fire by night, from before the people.

Spirit is Power
Ye shall receive power, after that the Holy Ghost (Spirit) is come upon you: And ye shall be witnesses unto me both in Jerusalem, and in all Judaea, and in Samaria, and unto the uttermost part of the earth.

Holy Spirit is our Teacher
The Comforter, which is the Holy Ghost (same as Spirit), whom the Father will send in my name, He shall teach you all things, and bring all things to your remembrance, whatsoever I have said unto you.

Holy Spirit is a Witness
When the Comforter is come, whom I will send unto you from the Father, even the Spirit of truth, which proceeded from the Father, He shall testify of me: And Ye also shall bear witness, because ye (the apostles) have been with me from the beginning.

That the blessing of Abraham might
Come on the Gentiles through Jesus
Christ; that we might receive the
Promise of the Spirit through faith.

Galatians 3:14

Holy Spirit as a Convincer (Convicts of Sin)
It is the Spirit that quickeneth; when He is come, He will reprove the world of sin, and righteousness, and of judgment . . . .

Holy Spirit is a Counselor
He shall glorify me (Jesus): for He shall receive of mine, and shall shew it unto you. He will shew you things to come.

Holy Spirit is a Speaker
Howbeit when he, the Spirit of truth, is come, he will guide you into all truth: for he shall not speak of himself; but whatsoever he shall hear, that shall he speak . . . .

Holy Spirit is Inspiration
For the prophecy came not in old time by the will of man: but holy men of God spake as they were moved by the Holy Ghost.

Holy Spirit as a Caller (To God's Assignments)
As they ministered to the Lord, and fasted, the Holy Ghost said, Separate me Barnabas and Saul for the work whereunto I have called them.

Holy Spirit as our Sender (To God's Field(s)
So they, being sent forth by the Holy Ghost, departed unto Seleucia; and from thence they sailed to Cyprus.

Holy Spirit as our Guard (Against Left Field(s))
Now when they had gone throughout Phrygia and the region of Galatia, and were forbidden of the Holy Ghost to preach the word in Asia. After they were come to Mysia, they assayed to go into Bithynia: but the Spirit suffered them not.

Holy Spirit is our Intercessor
Likewise the Spirit also helpeth our infirmities: for we know not what we should pray for as we ought: but the Spirit itself maketh intercession for us with groaning which cannot be uttered.

Now we have received, not the spirit
Of the world, but the Spirit which is of
God; that we might know the things
That are freely given to us of God.

1 Corinthians 2:12

Holy Spirit is our Comforter

For the Lord shall comfort Zion . . . (Through His Spirit, He does so.)In the multitude of my thoughts within me thy comforts (by His Spirit) delight my soul. I (Jesus Christ) will not leave you comfortless: I (Holy Spirit) will come to you. Who comforted us in all our tribulation, that we may be able to comfort them which are in any trouble, by the comfort wherewith we ourselves are comforted of God. (Through the Spirit of God.)

Our wholehearted praises to God Almighty for Pentecost: which bought on the complete phase of the Holy Spirit coming to us. The prophecy of Joel was fulfilled. And when the day of Pentecost was fully come, they were all with one accord in one place. And suddenly there came a sound from heaven as of a rushing mighty wind, and it filled all the house where they were sitting. And there appeared unto them cloven tongues like as of fire, and it sat upon each Of them. And they were all filled with the Holy Ghost, and began to speak with other tongues, as the Spirit gave them utterance.

Peter said, "But this is that which was spoken by the prophet Joel; 'And it shall come to pass in the last days, saith God, I will pour out of my Spirit upon all flesh: and your sons and your daughters shall prophesy, and your young men shall see visions, and your old men shall dream dreams: And on my servants and on my handmaidens I will pour out in those days of my Spirit; and they shall prophesy:' . . . Therefore (Jesus) being by the right hand of God exalted, and having received of the Father the promise of the Holy Ghost, He hath shed forth this, which ye now see and hear." The fulfillment of the Holy Spirit shed forth for us.

For there are three that bear record in heaven, the Father, the Word (Jesus Christ, the Word made flesh) and the Holy Ghost (Spirit): and these three Are **One.** Glory Hallelujah!

For God hath not given us the spirit of
Fear; but of power, and of love, and of
A sound mind.

2 Timothy 1:7

Thank you Most Wonderful Spirit of God.
AKJV: Genesis, Exodus, Numbers, Job, Psalm, Isaiah, The Gospels, Acts,
Romans, Corinthians, Ephesians.

But whosoever drinketh of the water
That I shall give him shall never thirst;
But the water that I shall give him
Shall be in him a well of water
Springing up into everlasting life.

John 4:14

TRULY BLESSED

Ask the Holy Spirit to speak to your spirit in order that you can receive all
The blessing, this lesson from Christ, has for you.

BLESSED ARE THE POOR IN SPIRIT:
FOR THEIRS IS THE KINGDOM OF HEAVEN.
BLESSED ARE THEY THAT MOURN:
FOR THEY SHALL BE COMFORTED.
BLESSED ARE THE MEEK:
FOR THEY SHALL INHERIT THE EARTH.
BLESSED ARE THEY WHICH DO HUNGER AND THIRST
AFTER RIGHTEOUSNESS:
FOR THEY SHALL BE FILLED.
BLESSED ARE THE MERCIFUL:
FOR THEY SHALL OBTAIN MERCY.
BLESSED ARE THE PURE IN HEART:
FOR THEY SHALL SEE GOD.
BLESSED ARE THE PEACEMAKERS:
FOR THEY SHALL BE CALLED THE CHILDREN OF GOD.
BLESSED ARE THEY WHICH ARE PERSECUTED FOR
RIGHTEOUSNESS'SAKE:
FOR THEIRS IS THE KINGDOM OF HEAVEN.
BLESSED ARE YE, WHEN MEN SHALL REVILE YOU, AND
PERSECUTE YOU, AND SHALL SAY ALL MANNER OF EVIL
AGAINST YOU FALSELY, FOR MY SAKE.
REJOICE, AND BE EXCEEDING GLAD:
FOR GREAT IS YOUR REWARD IN HEAVEN:
FOR SO PERSECUTED THEY THE PROPHETS WHICH WERE
BEFORE YOU.

My fruit is better than gold, yea, than
Fine gold; and my revenue than choice
Silver.

Proverbs 8:19

Matthew 5.
AKJV

Blessed shalt thou be when thou
Comest in, and blessed shalt thou be
When thou goest out.

Deuteronomy 28:6

THE BIBLE

This book reveals the mind of God; the state of man; the way of salvation; the doom of sinners; and the happiness of believers.

Its doctrines are holy; its precepts are binding; its histories are true; and its decisions are immutable.

Read it to be wise; believe it to be safe; and practice it to be holy. It contains light to direct you; food to support you; and comfort to cheer you.

It is the travelers map; the pilgrim's staff; the pilot's compass; the soldier's sword; and the Christian's charter. Here, too, heaven is opened, and the gates of hell disclosed.

Christ is its grand subject; our good, its design; and the glory of God its end.

It should fill the memory; rule the heart; and guide the feet. Read it slowly, frequently, prayerfully; it is a mine of wealth; a paradise of glory; and a river of pleasure.

It is given you in life; will be opened at the judgment; and be remembered forever; it involves highest responsibility; will reward the greatest labor; and condemn all who trifle with its sacred contents.

Owned, it is riches; studied, it is wisdom; trusted, it is salvation; loved, it is character; and obeyed, it is power.

If ye know these things, happy are ye
If ye do them.

John 13:17

Author Unknown

The Lord gave the word: great was
The company of those that published
It.

Psalm 68:11

MILK-N-HONEY

In that day, I lifted up mine hand unto them, to bring them forth of the land of Egypt into a land that I had espied for them, flowing with milk and honey, which is the glory of all lands: . . . I am the LORD your God. It shall come to pass in that day, that the mountains shall drop down new wine, and the hills shall flow with milk, and all the rivers of Judah shall flow with waters, and a fountain shall come forth of the house of the LORD, (watering).

Milk: one of the nutritive material taken into a living organism to sustain life, to promote growth and the repair of the tissues, and to give energy for the vital process.*
Honey: honey is a standard of comparison for pleasant things*; honey is the quality or state of being sweet; sweetness.**

No wonder the terms "milk-n-honey" was so often used to characterize a deliverance of God's people. No better term, I know, can describe the great deliverances done in our lives by God Almighty.

And the Word was made flesh, and dwelt among us (and we beheld His glory, the glory as of the only begotten of the Father,) full of **grace** and **truth.** (A More Perfect **Milk-n-Honey).**
Much more then, being now **justified** by His blood, we shall be saved from the wrath (judgment) through him. (A More Perfect **Milk-n-Honey**). Unto Him that **loved** us, and **washed** us from our sins in his own blood, and hath made us kings and priests unto God and His Father; to Him be glory and dominion for ever and ever. A-men. (Much More Perfect **Milk-n-Honey,** huh?)

Trust in the LORD, and do good; so
Shalt thou dwell in the land, and verily
Thou shalt be fed.

Psalm 37:3

Apostle John said also: And I went unto the angel, and said unto him, Give me the little book. And he said unto me, Take it, and eat it up; and it shall make thy belly (flesh) bitter, but it shall be in thy mouth sweet as honey. And I took the little book out of the angel's hand, and ate it up; and it was in my mouth sweet as honey . . . .

King David declared about the statues of God: More to be desired are they than gold, yea, than much fine gold: sweeter also than honey and the honeycomb. How sweet are thy words unto my taste! Yea, sweeter than honey to my mouth. (Better Than The Best **Milk-n-Honey**).

GREAT ARE THY TENDER MERCIES, O LORD. THANK YOU FATHER, THANK YOU SON, AND THANK YOU HOLY SPIRIT. THANK YOU FOR OUR **MILK-N-HONEY**.

Passages from AKJV: Old & New Testament.
*Definition from *The Zondervan Bible Dictionary*.
**From Webster New Collegiate Dictionary*.

Fear not, little flock; for it is your
Father's good pleasure to give you the
Kingdom.

Luke 12:32

REAL LOVE

As we strive toward perfection in love*

Set your mind on the higher gifts. And now I am going to put before you the best way of all.

Though I command languages both human and angelic—if I speak without
Love,
I am no more than a gong booming or a cymbal clashing
And though I have the power of prophecy, to penetrate all mysteries and knowledge, and though I have all the faith necessary to move mountains—if I am without
Love,
I am nothing. Though I should give away to the poor all that I possess, and even give up my body to be burned—if I am without
love,
It will do me no good whatever.

Love
Is always patient and kind;
Love
Is never jealous;
Love
Is not boastful or conceited, it is never rude and never seeks its own advantage, it does not take offence or store up grievances.
Love
Does not rejoice at wrongdoing, but finds its joy in the truth. It is always ready to make allowances, to trust, to hope and to endure whatever comes.
Love
Never comes to an end. But if there are prophecies, they will be done away

For God so loved the world, that he
Gave his only begotten Son, that
Whosoever believeth in him should
Not perish, but have everlasting life.

John 3:16

With; if tongues, they will fall silent; and if knowledge, it will be done away with. For we know only imperfectly, and we prophesy imperfectly; but once perfection comes, all imperfect things will be done away with. When I was a child, I used to talk like a child, and see things as a child does, and think like a child; but now that I have become an adult, I have finished with all childish ways. Now we see only reflections in a mirror, mere riddles, but then we shall be seeing face to face. Now, I can know only imperfectly; but then I shall know just as fully as I am myself known.

As it is, these remain: faith, hope and
love,
The three of them; and the greatest of them is
love.

*The NJ Bible, October, 2010.
Glory to our merciful God almighty!

The LORD hath appeared of old unto
Me, saying, yea, I have loved thee
With an everlasting love: therefore
With lovingkindness have I drawn
Thee.

Jeremiah 31:3

SEEKING THE KINGDOM OF GOD

(A Message for Believers)

Matthew 6:33
Seek ye first the kingdom of God, and His righteousness; and all these things shall be added unto you.

And gave for the service of the house of God of gold five thousand talents and ten thousand drams, and of silver ten thousand talents, and of brass eighteen thousand talents, and one hundred thousand talents of iron. And they with whom precious stones were found gave them to the treasure of the house of the LORD, . . .
Then the people rejoiced, for that they offered willingly, because with perfect heart they offered willingly to the LORD: and David the king also rejoiced with great joy. (From 1 Chr. 29.)

There was nothing incorrect with the offerings made by the Israelites with a willing heart to God. However, there's something much more important in our duties to the Lord. So much more important is it to find the kingdom of God. It is more valuable than all the gold, silver, bronze, iron, or any other precious stones or items to us.

There had always been a longing for the coming of the Messiah who should establish his just and peaceful rule over the people of God, which would endure forever. Here is a new covenant which is given to a people who have surrendered their hearts to God and received his forgiving grace: "Behold

That they should seek the LORD, if
Happily they might feel after him, and
Find him, though he be not far from
Every one of us . . .

Acts 17:27

the days are coming, saith God, that I will make with the house of Israel and with the house of Judah a new covenant; not like the covenant which I made with their fathers in the day when I took them by the hand to bring them out of the land of Egypt—which covenant of mine they broke though I was a husband to them, saith God. But this is the covenant which I will make with the house of Israel after those days, saith God: I will put my law within them, and on their heart will I write it; and I will be their God, and they shall be my people. And no more shall they teach each his neighbor and each his brother saying, 'Know God.' For all of them shall know me, from the least to the greatest of them, saith God; for I will forgive their iniquity, and their sin will I remember no more." (From Jer. 31.)

The gospels make it quite clear that the teaching and preaching of Christ Jesus was to announce the Kingdom of God. And victoriously did He announce it! Jesus said, "The Kingdom of God is Here". Jesus came into Galilee, preaching the gospel of the kingdom of God, and saying, "The time is fulfilled, and the kingdom of God is at hand: repent ye, and believe the Gospel." (From Mark 1.) Jesus went throughout the cities and villages preaching and shewing (proclaiming) the glad tidings of the kingdom of God with His followers. Jesus said, "But if I with the finger of God cast out devils, no doubt the kingdom of God is come upon you." Jesus told the Pharisees that the kingdom of God cometh not with observation, therefore, It cannot be said it is here or there; for, behold, the kingdom of God is within you.

The Apostle Paul expounds on the Kingdom even further; when he tells the Roman Church that the kingdom of God is righteousness, and peace, and Joy in the Holy Ghost. As told to the Hebrews, we have received a Kingdom which cannot be moved. The Apostle John heard a loud voice come down from heaven saying, "NOW IS COME SALVATION, AND STRENGTH, AND THE KINGDOM OF OUR GOD, AND THE POWER OF HIS CHRIST". Glory, Glory, Glory Hallelujah!

But if from thence thou shalt seek the
LORD thy God, thou shalt find him, if
Thou seek him with all thy heart and
With all thy soul.

Deuteronomy 4:29

Direct quotes from the AKJV Bible
Thank you Holy Ghost!

The LORD is good unto them that
Wait for him, to the soul that seeketh
Him.

Lamentations 3:25

ABUNDANTLY BLESSED

Blessed are the peacemakers.
Are all the saints peacemakers? Selah.
Blessed are the apostles.
Are all saints apostle? Selah.
Blessed are God's pastors.
Do all the saints under shepherd a church?
Blessed are God's teachers.
Are all saints gifted to teach?
Blessed are Christ's fathers.
Are all God's gentlemen dads?
Blessed are Christ's mothers.
Are all God's ladies mothers?
Blessed are God's gifted helpers.
Are all saints blessed with the gift of helps?
Blessed are God's singers and musicians.
Do we all play and sing with harmony?
Blessed are God's writers.
Are all the saints authors?
Blessed are God's business owners.
Are we all entrepreneurs?
Blessed are God's home and land owners.
Do we all have homeowner deeds?
Blessed are the gifted ones with a word of wisdom.
Do all speak with understanding?
Blessed are the spiritually gifted with a word of encouragement.
Do we all have the gift of exhortation?

Praise God for diverse blessings.
Praise the Lord for abundant blessings.

I will abundantly bless her provision:
I will satisfy her poor with bread.

Psalm 132:15

Praise our Creator for daily, showers of blessings.

A Soldier of Christ, 1998.

Be glad then, ye children of Zion, and
Rejoice in the LORD your God: for he
Hath given you the former rain, and
The latter rain in the first month.
And the floors shall be full of wheat,
And the fats shall overflow with wine
And oil.

Joel 2:23

WHOSOEVER WILL CAN COME

(A Message of Salvation)

Ro. 10:9, 10

That if thou shalt confess with thy mouth the Lord Jesus, and shalt believe in thine heart that God hath raised him from the dead, thou shalt be saved. For with the heart man believeth unto righteousness, and with the mouth confession is made unto salvation.

Now let's take a glance with spiritual eyes. Someone is lying there in distraught with bars surrounding their habitant; wondering where did they go wrong in life. At another location, there's another person sitting on a bar stool, staring into the container from which you are drinking; gazing from one to the other of the people in which you accompany; deciding the move of your next direction. Another person is devastated because their marriage has failed and neither party can figure out who is really at fault. And sadly, there in an ally, is someone who cannot see how to take another step; because, their body is so consumed with drugs.

Not a pretty picture at all; however, there is still hope. For God word says to us, "while we were yet sinners, Christ died for us," still. We are all sinners by nature first; then afterward, by choice. The Word of God says, "For all have sinned, and come short of the glory of God". (Ro. 3:23).

The reason we do not have to remain in the state of being distraught, confused, devastated, misdirected, or just plain lost; is because Jesus took those sins of ours to the cross. First Peter 3:18 says, "For Christ also hath once suffered for sins, the just for the unjust, that He might bring us to God, being put to death in the flesh, but quickened by the Spirit:" Jesus died so that we may have life in the Spirit of God. "Who (Jesus) was delivered for our offences over to death for our sins) and was raised again (to life) for

Jesus answered and said unto him,
Verily, verily, I say unto thee, Except
You be born again, you cannot see the
Kingdom of God.

John 3:3

our justification": Ro. 4:25.

You may not know what to do or say, but you can know, that God loves you, still, and has a purpose for your life, still. John 3:16 tells us, "For God so loved the world that he gave his only begotten Son, that whosoever believeth in him should not perish, but have everlasting life". God has given us the free gift of life. We make the choice to either accept that gift of abundant life, or to reject that gift, by destroying our lives. Romans 6:23
Clearly tells us "For the wages of sin is death (spiritual death first); but the gift of God is eternal life through Jesus Christ our Lord." Jesus told us in John 10:10 that, "I am come that they might have life, and that they might have it more abundantly."

The next move, then, is to turn to God through belief (faith) in Jesus Christ and confess that belief. Romans 10:9: "That if thou shalt confess with thy mouth the Lord Jesus, and shalt believe in thine heart that God hath raised Him from the dead, thou shalt be saved."

Now that the decision to turn to God has been made, the power of repentance, by the Holy Spirit of God, has set to working. "Repent therefore, and be converted, that your sins may be blotted out". (Acts 3:19).
Go tell someone that you believe the Lord Jesus Christ is truly in your heart and life, right now. Conclusively, go wash in the Word. (Jesus said, "Go wash in the pool of Siloam," Jn. 9:7). Attend believers assemblies; learn of God; attend church.

Hallelujah to God Almighty; you have received the salvation of HIM through Jesus Christ, our Lord! Praise ye the LORD!

Thank you Holy Spirit of God.

For this is good and acceptable in the
Sight of God our Saviour; who will
Have all men to be saved, and to come
Unto the knowledge of the truth.

1 Timothy 2:3,4

KEEPING YOUR HEAD ABOVE WATERS

(A Message for Believers)

Isaiah 8:5-8

The LORD spake also unto me again, saying, forasmuch as this people refuseth the waters of Shiloah that go softly, and rejoice in Rezin and Remaliah's son; now therefore, behold, the Lord bringeth up upon them the waters of the river, strong and many, even the king of Assyria, and all his glory: and he shall come up over all his channels, and go over all his banks: and he shall pass through Judah; he shall overflow and go over, he shall reach even to the neck; and the stretching out of his wings shall fill the breadth of thy land, O Immanuel.

On occasion, a boater may capsize out in the middle of a river. When swimming out of the deep waters, his main objective in getting to land is keeping his head above the water.

In the eighth chapter of the book of Isaiah is a lesson about a people who gets in deep waters. It was written after the Israelites split into the two divisions: the children of Israel and the other, the children of Judah.

The people refused the water of Shiloah that went calm and softly; they despised their own territory (their pool of Siloam), and loved running it down. Is that why some today would rather watch church service on internet or television rather than be in the assembly of worship service? Because their land did not make so great a noise in the world, as some other lands did? The waters God had given them in Shiloah weren't enough for the people. They admired the great river Euphrates of Assyria and rejoiced in Rezin and Remaliah's son. These were another king and kingdom who were actually the people's enemy. Remaliah's son was Pekah, a king of Israel who

If any of thine be driven out unto the
Outmost parts of heaven, from thence
Will the LORD thy God gather thee,
And from thence will he fetch thee . . .

Deuteronomy 30:4

had betrayed God's Kingdom by allying himself with king Rezin (the enemy) against part of God's Kingdom (that Jotham, king of Judah had continued to establish).

Well king Ahaz admired the river Euphrates so much, until it got up to his neck.
II Chr. 28:22 And in the time of his distress did he trespass yet more against The LORD: this is that king Ahaz.

Therefore, when the church of God allies with current Rezin(s) and Pekah(s), it is still Immanuel's Land. When the church of God allies with those who talk falsely and maliciously about the land, it is still the Land of Christ Jesus. When we allow the enemy, current Assyria, to ally with us, we are still God's Land, Hallelujah! No matter what is attempted to be done to us, as God's Land, we can always look to our LORD and SAVIOR JESUS CHRIST, the KING OF KINGS. God will keep our heads above waters. For in the time of trouble he shall hide me in his pavilion, in the secret of His tabernacle shall he hide me; he shall set me up upon a rock. Ps. 27:5.
I will be glad and rejoice in thy mercy; for thou hast considered my trouble; Thou hast known my soul in adversities; And hast not shut me up into the hand of the enemy: thou hast set my feet in a large room. Ps. 31: 7,8.
The LORD also will be a refuge for the oppressed, a refuge in times of trouble. Ps. 9:9. Praise God Almighty!

Whether there is trouble in our lives, our marriages, with the younger ones, with siblings or parents, in illnesses or addictions which are caused by the lust of the flesh, the lust of the eye, or the pride of life; just knowing our Savior is there to deliver, is priceless. On the other hand, contrary to this story about king Ahaz, our troubles that sometimes get up to our necks, are due to no fault of our own; but are caused by the enemy (consider Job or the Apostle Paul). Still, JEHOVAH-NISSI is right there as our banner. When God be for us, who can be against us (against Him)? Our LORD, who loves us unconditionally; our MOST HIGH GOD, who sits high and sees all, is right there. Thank God almighty! What Peace! What blessed assurance!

What shall we render unto the LORD for all His goodness toward us?
1.   Thanksgiving
       II Cor. 9:15 Thanks be unto God for his unspeakable gift.
       Ps. 147:7 Sing unto the Lord with thanksgiving; sing praise upon the harp

The LORD shall preserve thy going
Out and thy coming in from this time
Forth, and even for evermore.

Psalm 121:8

unto our God.

2.   Praise
Heb. 13:15 By him therefore let us offer the sacrifice of praise to God continually, that is, the fruit of our lips giving thanks to his name. Ps. 150:2 Praise him for his mighty acts: praise him for his excellent greatness.

3.   Sacrifices of Joy
Ps. 27:6 . . . therefore will I offer in his tabernacle sacrifices of joy . . . Phil 4:4 Rejoice in the Lord always; and again I say, rejoice.

4.   Sacrifices of Good Deeds
Heb. 13:16 But to do good and to communicate forget not: for with such sacrifices God is well pleased.
IICor. 9:7, 12 Every man according as he purposeth in his heart, so let him give; not grudgingly, or of necessity: for God loveth a cheerful giver. For the administration of this service not only supplieth the want of the saints, but is abundant also by many thanksgiving unto God . . . .

Thank you God for the light of our Lord and Savior Jesus Christ and the Sweet communion of the Holy Spirit. Praise ye the Lord!

Glory to the Holy Spirit; Initiated during Seminary Class 1990's.

He brought them out of darkness and
The shadow of death, and brake their
Bands in sunder.

Psalm 107:14

WAIT ON IT

Romans 8:24-25
For we are saved by hope: but hope that is seen is not hope: for what a man seeth, why doth he yet hope for? But if we hope for that we see not, then do we with patience wait for it.

<u>Examples of waiting times</u>

     1.   Waiting in line
          A.   Employment line
          B.   Cafeteria line
          C.   Ticket line
          D.   Shopping line
     2.   Waiting for a house to close
     3.   Waiting to receive an imbursement in the mail.

<u>People who waited</u>

1. Noah waited for the rain to start and stop.
2. Joseph waited for deliverance from the well, from prison, and to see his father and family again.
3. Gideon waited for signs from God to confirm his calling.
4. Hannah waited on her son, Samuel.
5. Hezekiah waited for the Lord to deliver him from an illness unto death.
6. Deborah waited on the victory, from God, over her many enemies.
7. Daniel waited 15 days to receive the answer from his prayer.
8. Job, one of the best examples of waiting on the Lord, waited through much suffering.
   Job said in Job 14:14: . . . All the days of my appointed time will I

And let us not be weary in well doing:
For in due season we shall reap,
If we faint we faint not.

Galatians 6:9

wait, till my change come.

9. Mary waited for God to deliver their hearts after Jesus was crucified.
10. Apostle Paul waited so many times on the Lord for deliverance from prison, beatings, from a shipwreck, robbers, from false brethren, from weariness, from pain, from watchings often, from hunger, thirst, from dangers caused by his own people, from dangers caused by the unsaved, and from perils in the wilderness and the sea. Through it all, Apostle Paul still had the job to care for the church started in each location. He kept the faith and finished his course.

How could God's people do all this? How could they time after time keep waiting on the Lord? How can we?

Why should we wait on the Lord? Because God said wait.
Ps. 27;14 Wait on the Lord . . . wait, I say on the Lord.
Ps. 37:34 Wait on the Lord, and keep His way . . .

How should we wait on Him?

1. Boldly
    Ps. 25:3 Yea, let none that wait on thee be ashamed: let them be ashamed which transgress without a cause.
2. Courageously
    Ps. 27:14 Wait on the Lord: be of good courage, and he shall strengthen thine heart: wait, I say, on the Lord.
3. Patiently
    Ps. 37:7 Rest in the Lord, and wait patiently for him . . .
4. Uprightly
    Ps. 37:34 Wait on the Lord, and keep His way . . .
5. Prayerfully
    I Co. 9:13 . . . they which wait at the altar are partakers with the altar. After waiting boldly, courageously, patiently, prayerfully, and uprightly on the Lord, His promise to us is that we will experience result(s) from the wait. Some examples:

Be patient therefor, brethren, unto
The coming of the Lord. Behold, the
Husbandman waited for the precious
Fruit of the earth, and hath long
Patience for it, until he receive the
Early and latter rain.
Be ye also patient; stablish your
Hearts: for the coming of the Lord
Draweth nigh.

James 5:7,8

1. Renewed strength
   Is. 40:31 But they that wait upon the Lord shall renew their strength . . .
   Ps. 59:9 Because of His strength will I wait upon thee: for God is my
   Defence.
2. Blessings
   Is. 30:18 . . . blessed are all they that wait for him.
   Lam. 3:25 The Lord is good unto them that wait for him . . .
   Gal. 6:9 And let us not be weary in well doing: for in due season we
   Shall reap, if we faint not.
3. Righteousness shall prevail
   Gal. 5:5 For we through the Spirit wait for the hope of righteousness
   By faith.
4. Protection
   Prov. 20:22 Say not thou, I will recompense evil; but wait on the Lord
   and he shall save thee.
   Rom. 12:19 Dearly beloved, avenge not yourselves, but rather give
   Place unto wrath: for it is written, vengeance is mine; I will repay,
   Saith the Lord.
5. An answer
   Ps. 40:1 David said, "I waited patiently for the Lord; and he inclined
   Unto me, and heard my cry.
   Acts 18:9 Then spake the Lord to Paul by a night vision, Be not
   Afraid, but speak, and hold not thy peace.

The precious Holy Spirit, God gave unto us through His Son, Jesus Christ,
sustains us. So we thank God, through Christ Jesus, for each wait. Hallelujah
to God Almighty, as we wait for Christ's second coming in the rapture. What
a truly, awesome time that will be, praise ye the Lord!

But he that shall endure unto the end,
The same shall be saved.

Matthew 24:13

By Your Holy Spirit Lord, P. Cook

Let us hold fast the profession of our
Faith without wavering; (for he is
Faithful that promised) . . .

Hebrews 10:23

GOD'S MIGHTY SPIRITUAL ANGELS

Angels are created, supernatural, heavenly beings that were before the creation of man. For example, Raphael, Gabriel, and Michael; among others created by God Almighty.

Representing God

And the angel of the LORD found her by a fountain of water in the wilderness, by the fountain in the way to Shur (her destination). And God heard the voice of the lad; and the angel of God called to Hagar out of heaven and said unto her, What aileth thee, Hagar?

And the angel of the LORD called unto him out of heaven, and said, Abraham, Abraham: and he said Here am I.

And there appeared an angel unto Him (Jesus) from heaven, strengthening him.

God's Messengers

And the angel answering said unto him, I am Gabriel, that stand in the presence of God; and am sent to speak unto thee, and to shew thee these glad tidings.

Behold, the angel of the LORD appeared unto him in a dream, saying, Joseph, thou son of David, fear not to take unto thee Mary thy wife; for that which is conceived in her is of the Holy Ghost.

And he said unto me, These sayings are faithful and true: and the Lord God of the holy prophets sent his angel to shew unto his servants the things which must shortly be done.

For the Lord himself shall descend
From heaven with a shout, with the
Voice of the archangel, and with the
Trump of God . . .

1 Thessalonians 4:16

Mediating Angels

I was sent to test your faith, and at the same time God sent me to heal you and your daughter-in-law Sarah. I am Raphael, one of the seven angels who stand ever ready to enter the presence of the glory of the LORD.

And, behold, the angel of the LORD came upon him, and a light shined in the prison: and he smote Peter on the side, and raised him up, saying, Arise up quickly, And his chains fell off from his hands.

. . . And it was ordained by angels in the hand of a mediator.

And it came to pass, as they were much perplexed thereabout, behold two angels stood by them (Mary and the other women) in shining garments . . . .

And the angel of the LORD spake unto Philip, saying, Arise, and go toward the south unto the way that goeth down from Jerusalem unto Gaza, which is the desert.

Guardian Angels

Behold, I send an angel before thee, to keep thee in the way, and to bring thee into the place which I have prepared.

For He shall give His angels charge over thee, to keep thee in all thy ways.

The angel of the LORD encampeth round about them that fear him, and saved him out of all his troubles.

Angels Encounters

Let me plainly share an angel experience of mine with you. It was late at night when the event occurred. I was driving back home from a visit with my biological mother and family. I became sleepy and dozed off for a few seconds. I awoke on the back end of a big-wheeler truck; however, thanks to an angel of God intervening, I mysteriously did not ram into the truck's rear end. My life was saved by God Almighty. Jesus said, "whosoever call upon

. . . Blessed be the God of Shadrach,
Meshach, and Abednego,who hath
Sent his angel, and delivered his
Servants that trusted in him . . .

Daniel 3:28

the name of the LORD shall be saved."

Even though my encounter with the angel of the LORD was spiritual; my earthly mother from the Spirit of God, declared actually seeing an angel of God. This most honorable lady of God taught Sunday School in church even into her nineties. She is the writer of "Prodigal Girl" which is included in this documentary. What an Almighty God we worship and praise. Bless the LORD GOD; thank you JESUS!

Worshipping Angels

And again, when He bringeth in the Firstbegotten into the world, He saith, And let all the angels of God worship Him.

And of the angels He saith, Who maketh His angels spirits, and His ministers a flame of fire.

And all the angels stood round about the throne, and about the elders and the four beasts, and fell before the throne on their faces, and worshipped God,
Saying, A-men: Blessing, and glory, and wisdom, and thanksgiving, and honour, and power, and might, be unto our God for ever and ever. A-men.

Victorious-in-Battle Angels

And there came two angels unto Sodom at even; . . . and he bowed himself with his face toward the ground.

And there was war in heaven: Michael and his angels fought against the dragon; and the dragon fought and his angels, and prevailed not; neither was their place found any more in heaven.

Hallelujah to God Almighty for Angels!

Through God we shall do valiantly:
For he it is that shall tread down our
Enemies.

Psalm 60:12

AKJV; NJ Bibles
October, 2010

For an angel went down at a certain
Season into the pool, and troubled
The water: whosoever then first after
The troubling of the water
Stepped in was made whole of
Whatsoever disease he had.

John 5:4

WHAT NAME DO YOU CALL CHRIST JESUS?

... WHOM DO MEN SAY THAT I THE SON OF MAN AM?
MT. 16:13.

JESUS CHRIST	ALL FOUR GOSPELS
WONDERFUL COUNSELOR	IS. 9:6
MIGHTY GOD	IS. 9:6
EVERLASTING FATHER	IS.9:6
PRINCE OF PEACE	IS.9:6
ROSE OF SHARON	SGS.OF SOL. 2:1
LILY OF THE VALLEY	SGS.OF SOL. 2:1
MASTER	JN. 4:31
PROPHET	JN.6:14
LORD	JN.6:34
SON OF JOSEPH	JN. 1:45
RABBI	JN. 3:2
JEW	JN. 4:9
MESSIAH	JN. 4;25, 26
SON OF GOD	MT. 16:16
THE CHRIST	MT. 16:16
SIR	JN. 4:11
SAVIOR	LK. 2:11
RABBONI	JN. 20:16
SON OF MAN	JN. 12:23
KING OF JEWS	JN. 18:39
KING	JN. 12:15
MIRACLE WORKER	JN. 11:47
GOOD SHEPHERD	JN. 10:11
GOOD MAN	JN. 7:12
SON OF THE LIVING GOD	JN. 6:69

OTHER NAMES CALLED OUR LORD FROM A FOUL SPIRIT: DECEIVER, UNKNOWLEDGED MAN, DEVIL, SUICIDAL, SAMARATAN DEVIL, SINNER, FELLOW, STRANGER, MAD, BELZEBUB, CHIEF DEVIL. (NAMES CALLED IN THE GOSPELS).

WE CALL CHRIST JESUS, THE SON OF GOD: OUR EVERLASTING SAVIOR!

BUT WHOM SAY YOU THAT I AM?
MT. 16:15
(AKJV)

And he hath on his vesture and on his
Thigh a name written, KING OF
KINGS, AND LORD OF LORDS.

Revelations 19:16

TESTIMONY OF "FOOTPRINTS"

An unknown writer wrote a passage similar to this, that has been read by countless household members.

One night I had a dream.
I dreamed I was walking along the beach with the LORD.
Across the sky flashed scenes from my life.
For each scene I noticed two sets of footprints in the sand.
One belonged to me, and the other belonged to the LORD.
When the last scene of my life flashed before me, I looked at the footprints
In the sand.
I noticed that many times along the path of my life, there was only one set of
Footprints.
I also noticed that it happened at the very lowest and saddest times in my '
Life.
This really bothered me, so I questioned the LORD about it.
LORD, you said that once I decided to follow you, you will walk with me
All the way.
But, I noticed that during the most troublesome times in my life, there is
Only one set of footprints.
I don't understand why you would leave me, LORD.
The LORD replied, my precious, precious child.
During your times of trial and suffering, when you saw only one set of
Footprints;
IT WAS THEN THAT I CARRIED YOU.

Sometimes, when I reflect back on my life: past and present trials and sufferings, I thank CHRIST JESUS. I thank HIM for bringing me out. nobody can do us like JESUS. It does not matter whether you are addicted to drugs, alcohol, sex or any other addiction; HE can carry you out, if you

. . . The beloved of the LORD shall
Dwell in safety by him; and the LORD
Shall cover him all the day long, and
He shall dwell between his shoulders.

Deuteronomy 33:12

want to be made whole. It does not matter if you are an adulterer or adulteress; HE will carry you, if you are willing to be made whole. You can be a killer, a prostitute, a pimp, a drug dealer, or an abuser; HE will deliver you out, when you surrender your will in faith to HIM. CHRIST JESUS OF NAZARETH came to heal the sick. HE came to set the captives free from spiritual bondage. ALLELUIA! HE came so that we can truly be the children of GOD ALMIGHTY.

Do you know HIM?
Won't HE do it for you?
If you have not really tried HIM, try JESUS today.
HE is our REDEEMER.
PRAISE YE THE LORD!

Romans 10:13
For whosoever shall call upon the name of the Lord shall be saved.

Glory to the MOST, HOLY SPIRIT OF GOD ALMIGHTY.

The LORD is my light and my
Salvation;
Whom shall I fear? The LORD is the
Strength of my life; of whom shall I
Be afraid?

Psalm 27:1

CHAPTER TWO

POEMS AND SONG LYRICS

THANK GOD FOR JESUS

THANK GOD FOR JESUS, GOOD FRIEND OF MINE
SELDOM IS FRIENDSHIP SUCH AS THINE
HOW VERY MUCH I LONG TO BE
AS HELPFUL AS YOU HAVE BEEN TO ME
WHEN I REMEMBER FROM TIME TO TIME
HOW YOU INSPIRED THIS HEART OF MINE
I FIND MYSELF COMPELLED TO SAY
GOD BLESS MY FRIEND JESUS EACH NEW DAY
SO OFTEN AT THE THRONE OF GRACE
I LONG TO SEE YOUR HOLY FACE
SOMEDAY, I HOPE WITH OTHERS TO STAND
PRAISING YOU JESUS AT GOD'S RIGHT HAND
AND TO SAY MOST JOYFULLY AT MY JOURNEY'S END
O ALLELUIA! I'M FINALLY WITH MY FRIEND.

November, 2010
Pro. 18:24

A man that hath friends must shew himself friendly: and there is a friend that
sticketh closer than a brother.
Jn. 15:13
Greater love hath no man than this, that a man lay down his life for his friends.
AKJV.

THANK YOU JESUS!

But if we walk in the light, as he is in
The light, we have fellowship one with
Another, and the blood of Jesus Christ
His Son cleanseth us from all sin.

1 John 1:7

GOT MY EYES ON THE PRIZE

(Song Lyrics)

Though a great company sometimes come up against us,
Still got my eyes on the prize.

It sometimes seem like the enemy is winning the battle,
Still got my eyes on the prize.

When the wicked fall into their own nets and we escape,
Still got my eyes on the prize.

Over and over you pluck our feet out of their nets,
Keeping our eyes on the prize.

O God the Lord, our eyes are unto thee, unto thee dear Lord,
We got our eyes on the prize.

O Lord, you told us to let our eyes look right on,
We got our eyes on the prize.

And let our eyelids look straight on before thee, almighty One,
Still keeping our eyes on the prize.

With our eyes ever toward you, O great Jehovah our Savior,
Still keeping our eyes on the prize.

While the builders rejected, Christ Jesus became the Head Stone,
Every keeping our eyes on the prize.

O God our Lord, our eyes are unto thee, unto thee dear Lord,
Got my eyes on the LORD GOD.
Got my eyes on the LORD GOD.

I press toward the mark for the prize
Of the high calling of God in Christ
Jesus.

Philippians 3:14

Got my eyes on the LORD GOD!

. . . And it is marvelous in our eyes.
Mt. 21:42b.

Wherefore we labour, that, whether
Present or absent, we may be accepted
Of HIM.

2 Corinthians 5:9

A PLACE IN HEAVEN

Our prayers have all been answered; I finally arrived.
The healing that had been delayed, has now been realized.
No one's in a hurry. There's no schedule to keep.
We're all enjoying JESUS; just sitting at His feet.

If you could see me now; I'm walking streets of gold.
If you could see me now; I'm standing tall and bold.
If you could see me now; you'd know I've seen His face.
If you could see me now; you'd know the pain is erased.
You wouldn't want me to ever leave this place;
If you could see me now.

Rev.21

And the twelve gates were twelve pearls; every several gate was of one
Pearl: and the street of the city was pure gold, as it were transparent glass.
And I saw no temple therein: for the Lord God Almighty and the Lamb are
The temple of it.

A.U./Received 2000.

We know that if our earthly house of
This tabernacle were dissolved, we
Have a building of God, an house not
Made with hands, eternal in heavens.

2 Corinthians 5:1

KEPT BY THE LORD'S ALMIGHTY POWER

(Song lyrics)

No longer are we weakened
No longer are we living in fear
No longer are we discouraged.

Because the Holy Spirit left here by our Lord and Savior Jesus Christ:

He strengthens us when we become weak
He gives us peace when there arises confusion
He gives us hope when situations suggest despair
And He restores our joy when sorrow tries to overcome us.

Sing alleluia, alleluia, alleluia Lord God Almighty
You keep blessing us and keeping us
Sing alleluia, alleluia, alleluia Lord God Almighty
Lord, You keep blessing us and keeping us.

Thank you Lord God
Thank you for salvation in Christ Jesus
Thank you Blessed Savior.

Penned December, 2000.

Is. 43:2 When thou passest through the waters, I will be with thee: and through the rivers, they shall not overflow thee: when thou walkest through the fire, thou shalt not be burned; neither shall the flame kindle upon thee. For I am the LORD thy God, the Holy one . . . , thy Savior . . .

They that trust in the LORD shall be
As mount Zion, which cannot be
Removed,
But abideth forever.

Psalm 125:1

TRUST HIM

Trust Him when doubts assail thee
Trust Him when thy strength seem small
Trust Him when to simply trust Him
Seems the hardest thing of all.

Trust Him, He is ever faithful
Trust Him, His perfect will is best
Trust Him, for thy Father's bosom
Is thy surest place to rest.

Trust Him in storm or sunshine
All thy cares upon Him cast
Until this term of life is over
And thy earthly days are past.

Author Unknown
Is. 26:4 Trust ye in the LORD for ever: for in the LORD JEHOVAH is
Everlasting strength.

Trust in the LORD with all thine
Heart; and lean not unto thine own
Understanding.

Proverbs 3:5

YOU GAVE US LOVE

(To JESUS, Our Testimony of Your Goodness)
(Lyrics to a song)

You gave us time when nobody else came our way.
You heard our dreams when others looked away.
You smiled at us when frowns seemed everywhere.
You gave us love when nobody gave us a prayer.

And that's why we can call you our Savior.
That's why we can call you our friend.
You touched our heart and changed our soul.
Helped us start over again.
That's why we love you Jesus.
That's why we'll always care.
You gave us love when nobody gave us a prayer.

You gave us laughter after we cried all our tears.
You heard our screams while others closed their ears.
We looked in your eyes and found the tenderness there.
You gave us love when nobody gave us a prayer.

That's why we call you our Savior.
That's why we call you our Friend.
You touched our heart and changed our soul.
Helped us start over again.
That's why we love you Jesus.
That's why we'll always care.
You gave us love when nobody gave us a prayer.
Yes you gave me love when nobody gave me a prayer.

We love him, because he first loved
Us.

1 John 4:19

Author Unknown

For the Father himself loveth you,
Because ye have loved me, and have
Believed that I came out from God.

John 16:27

WHAT OF THE PRODIGAL GIRL

We all have a heart for the prodigal boy.
Who was caught in sin's mad whirl.
And we welcome him back with songs of joy.
But what of the prodigal girl?

For the prodigal boy, there is an open door.
And a father's home bounteous fare.
Though he is wretched, sick, and poor.
He's sure of a welcome there.

But what of the girl who has gone astray.
Who got lost in the battle of sin.
Do we forgive in the same sweet way.
As always was forgiven him.

Does the door stand ajar as if to say.
Come enter; you need not fear.
I've been open since you went away.
Now close to a second year.

Or do we with hands of hellish pride.
Close and bolt the door.
And swear while Heaven and earth abide.
She will enter here no more.

Oh Lord, It seems we have never learned.
Your lesson taught in the sand.
For even yet the woman is spurned.
And stoned in a Christian land.

Down into the slough, we hurl her back.
Then turn around with a smile.

I will heal their backsliding, I will
Love them freely . . .

Hosea 14:4

Welcome the boy at the sinful track.
Though he being much more vile.

But what of the prodigal girl?

Susie Shields

Acts 2:17

And it shall come to pass in the last days, saith God, I will pour out of my
Spirit upon all flesh: and your sons and your daughters shall prophesy . . .
Gal. 3:28
There is neither Jew nor Greek, there is neither bond nor free, there is
Neither male nor female: for ye are all one in Christ Jesus.

Herein is love, not that we loved God,
But that he loved us, and sent his Son
To be the propitiation for our sins.

1 John 4:10

SUSTAINING POWER

(Song Lyrics)

When alone
Sometimes we get frightened
Sometimes we get discouraged
Sometimes we even get wearied

But thank GOD for our precious COMFORTER
That same HOLY SPIRIT that told the Hebrews

"THE LORD BLESS US AND KEEP US: THE LORD MAKE HIS FACE
TO SHINE UPON US, AND BE GRACIOUS UNTO US: THE LORD
LIFT UP HIS COUNTENANCE UPON US, AND GIVE US PEACE".

Numbers 6.

(Chorus)

Peace LORD, holy peace
Peace JESUS, Sweet peace
And we thank you LORD, thank you LORD, thank you LORD!

Pearl Cook (1998)

For this God is our God for ever and
Ever: he will be our guide even unto
Death.

Psalm 48:14

WHO TOUCHED ME?

Glory and honor to the ALMIGHTY most high
The ONE, during my longsuffering, kept me.
When I departed from HIS holy place
The LORD saw the state of my being:
Helpless, hopeless, heartbroken, and in despair
Was the state in which I was found.

Hallelujah, to the LORD most high
Your arms were not too short
That you could not reach me
Neither, oh holy ONE
Were your ears too cluttered
That you could not hear my cry
Thank you, blessed SAVIOR
You were not too fragile to lift me
Nor most wonderful ONE
Were you ever too busy
To place me in your arms
And carry me in your bosom.

Who touched me? JESUS lifted me
Who touched me? JESUS carried me
Who touched me? JESUS kept me.

Pearl Cook

But the salvation of the righteous is of
The LORD: he is their strength in the
Time of trouble.

Psalm 37:39

And he put them all out, and took her by the hand, and called, saying.
"Maid, arise."
Luke 8:54

Come unto me, all ye that labour and
Are heavy laden, and I will give you
Rest.

Matthew 11:28

WHAT MANNER MAN IS THIS?

What manner man is this?
Who walks in the midst of a room
Says "peace, be still" and heavenly peace resume.

What manner man is this?
Whose there during the needy time
Not only provides water; HE also provides wine.

What manner man is this?
Who converses with strangers along the way
Tells them their life in that same hour of day.

What manner man is this?
When HIS children goes astray
Brings them back in the straight and narrow way.

What manner man is this?
When there is a spirit of infirmity
Looses you from the illness and gives victory.

What manner man is this?
When there were just two fishes and five loaves of bread
Allowed five thousand people to be thoroughly fed.

What manner man is this?
Even when we are snared in sin

And when he was come into the
House, the blind men came to him:
And Jesus saith unto them, Believe ye
That I am able to do this? They said
Unto him, Yea, Lord.
Then touched he their eyes, saying,
According to your faith be it unto
You.
And their eyes were opened.

Matthew 9:28,29,30

Can forgive us and restore our spirit within.

What manner man is this?
Though HE was nailed to a cross
Counted it by no means a loss.

What manner man is this?
When the wind tosses your ships
Calms the troubled sea with a parting of his lips.

What manner man is this?
That humbly came from above
JESUS CHRIST is HIS name, GOD'S SON of love.

Pearl Cook

And they feared exceedingly, and said one to another, What manner of man
Is this, that even the wind and the sea obey him?

Mark 4:41kjv

119

And his fame went throughout all
Syria; and they brought unto him all
Sick people that were taken with
Divers diseases and torments, and
Those which were possessed with
Devils, and those which were lunatic,
And those that had the palsy; and he
Healed them.

Matthew 4:23,24

SERENITY PRAYER

(A Family Prayer)

Another poem in countless homes, is the "Serenity Prayer". No one knows its author's name; however, it, too, belongs in our "Treasure Chest". It is a prayer for peace through God's power of helping us with decisions.

God grant
Me (Us)
The serenity
To accept the things
I (We)
Cannot change
The courage
To change the things
I (We)
Can
And the wisdom to know
The difference.

In the precious name of Christ Jesus, Amen.

Not unto Him that is able to do exceeding abundantly above all that we ask
or think according to the power that worketh in us.
Eph.3:20 AKJV

Be careful for nothing; but in every
Thing by prayer and supplication with
Thanksgiving let your requests be
Made known unto God.
And the peace of God, which passeth
All understanding, shall keep your
Hearts and minds through Christ
Jesus.

Philippians 4:6,7

CHAPTER THREE

SPECIAL CHILDREN

ALBHABET SONG

(For the Little Ones)

ABCDEFGHIJKLMNOPQRSTUVWXYZ.
Now we know our abc's; now lets sing them in Jesus with ease.

A is for *always;* Jesus said He is with us *always.*
B is for *baby*; a sweet *baby* was born that night.
C is for *Christ;* Jesus *Christ* was His name.
D is for *devil*; the *devil* is not good.
E is for *eternal;* we can have *eternal* life.
F is for *father*; our *father* loves us.
G is for *God*; *God* created the world.
H is for *Heaven; Heaven* will be our home.
I is for *into*; come *into* this place.
J is for *Jesus*; *Jesus* is in my heart.
K is for *keeps*; He *keeps* us safe.
L is for *love*; we should *love* each other.
M is for *mother*; my *mother* is terrific.
N is for *now; now* is the right time.
O is for *on*; hold *on* to my hand.
P is for *precious*; I am so *precious* to Him.
Q is for *quickly*; go *quickly* to tell the Gospel.
R is for *right;* the Spirit helps us to do *right.*
S is for *still*; be *still,* to listen.
T is for *table*; a *table* is prepared for us.
U is for *upper;* He's in the *upper* room.
V is for *victory*; God gives us the *victory.*
W is for *word*; My *Word* lasts forever.
X is for *Xerox*; *Xerox* the life of Jesus.
Y is for *year*; learn about the Lord all *year.*

Now therefore hearken unto me, O ye
Children: for blessed are they that
Keep my ways.
Hear instruction, and be wise, and
Refuse it not.

Proverbs 8:32,33

Z is for *zion*; there are sons and daughters in *Zion*.

We love Him, because He first loved us.
1 Jn. 4:19

The father of the righteous shall greatly rejoice: and he that begetteth a wise
child shall have joy of him.

Proverbs 23:24

THANKSGIVING

(For Our Younger Ones)

Ps. 95:2; 100:4
Let us come before His presence with thanksgiving, and make a joyful noise
Unto Him with psalms.
Enter into His gates with thanksgiving and into His courts with praise: be
Thankful unto Him, and bless His name.

Prayer or Song
Thank you LORD, for the world so sweet
Thank you LORD, for the food we eat
Thank you LORD, for the birds that sing
Thank you GOD, for everything.**

Give thanks to the LORD, for he is
Good;
His love endures forever.

1 Chronicles 16:34

Prayer

Thank you dear GOD for loving us.
Thank you dear GOD for your Son, JESUS.
Thank you dear GOD for our whole family.
Thank you dear GOD for our Church family.
Thank you dear GOD for our School family.
Thank you JEHOVAH JIREH, Our Provider*, for good health.
Thank you for our home, food, clothing, and nation.
Thank you for all the extra things: toys, fun, and smiles.
Help us to love you and each other more.
In the name of your Son, JESUS CHRIST, AMEN.

Prayer

The LORD watch between me and thee, when we are absent one from
Another.
Thank you LORD for watching over us.
In JESUS name, AMEN.

My heart leaps for joy and I will give
Thanks to him in song.

Psalm 28:7

Gen. 31:49; AKJV
*Explain: the Same One GOD.
**A.U.

Give thanks in all circumstances, for
This is God's will for you in Christ
Jesus.

1 Thessalonians 5:18

JESUS LOVES THE LITTLE CHILDREN

Matthew 19:13,14
Then were there brought unto him little children, that He should put His hands on them, and pray; and the disciples rebuked them. But Jesus said, Suffer little children, and forbid them not, to come unto me: for such is the kingdom of heaven.

While our Jesus walked on this earth, He taught many sayings and lessons to the many people who followed Him. He taught a lesson to the older people about the little ones that were there by the Jordan River, with the adults.

Some of the children there were brought to Jesus, by their Moms and Dads, so that He would bless them specially. The disciples saw this happening, and began to stop the older people from bringing the children to Jesus. The disciples probably thought Jesus had enough older people to teach and did not have enough time to bless the children; however, the disciples thought was not like Jesus' thoughts.

Jesus told the disciples to let the children come to Him! He did not say any specific child; therefore, all kinds of children were welcome to come unto Jesus. Negroid, Mongoloid, Caucasian, happy children, sad children, rich children, poor children, healthy children, crippled children, high IQ's, low IQ's: all children can come unto Jesus. Jesus loves you one and all; Jesus wants you to love Him, also.

You can show Jesus you love Him by reading His words in the Bible when you can. You can show Jesus you love Him by listening to His words from the Bible, at Church and at Home, when you hear them. One day, when you believe Jesus lives in your heart, you can show Him you love Him by telling someone that His Spirit lives in your heart. You can show Him by telling

And all thy children shall be taught of
The LORD; and great shall be the
Peace of thy children.

Isaiah 54:13

Him in prayer and doing good deeds in life. And finally, you can show Jesus you love Him by obeying your mother and father. For it is written in Bible, where the words of Jesus are, that you should listen to your parents' teachings. (Pr. 4:1; Pr. 1:8; Eph. 6:1)

Remember, God loves you most of all; He will always love you. Bless Ye the Lord.

Lesson from Matthew 19. AKJV.
Thank you Lord Jesus.

They send forth their little ones like a
Flock, and their children dance.

Job 21:11

THE B-I-B-L-E

(Sing to the tune of O McDonald Had a Farm)

OUR GOD'S WORD IS IN A BOOK
TE B-I-B-L-E
AND IN HIS BOOK THERE ARE SOME (PSALMS)
THE B-I-B-L-E
THERE WAS A (PSALM), (PSALM) HERE AND A (PSALM), (PSALM)
THERE
HERE A (PSALM), THERE A (PSALM), EVERYWHERE A (PSALM),
(PSALM).

(Go back to the top line, singing to the tune of O McDonald Had a Farm;
Replacing the word (PSALMS) with):

(PROPHETS)
(LESSONS)
(ANGELS)
(TEACHERS)
(PEOPLE)
(PRIESTS)

(Go as long as you like being creative with people, trees, sheep, etc.)

P. Cook

For the promise is unto you, and to
Your children, and to all that are afar
Off, even as many as the Lord our God
Shall call.

Acts 2:39

JESUS IS ALIVE, HOORAY!
JESUS IS RISEN, HALLELUJAH!

(A Lesson For God's Young Ones)

Jesus said "I am the good shepherd: the good shepherd give his life for the sheep." (discuss meaning; Jn. 10:11)

Jesus was born on earth to forgive us, to heal us, to love us, and to show us how to love one another. Jesus wanted to help us and teach us how to live to please His father God and our God.

Some of the people did not like Jesus; they had their own little reasons not to like Jesus. They had no good reason not to like God's Son. Therefore, they set out to take Jesus away from them. They nailed Him to the cross and let him get buried. (discuss about losing something dear to you)

Now, the friends of Jesus were very sad and confused. They missed Jesus so much. They had forgotten that Jesus had told them what would happen to Him. The Holy Spirit has to remind us of God's plan in our lives.

Thank God, it was not over, though. On the third day, friends of Jesus went to the tomb (discuss) looking for Jesus. An angel told them Jesus was no longer in the tomb, but, Jesus has risen as He said He would. It was hard for them to believe it, at first; however, later, Jesus told them himself that He had risen and that He was alive forever. Because we love and believe Him, one day we will live with Jesus, forever. Hooray and Hallelujah to God!

And this is the record, that God hath
Given to us eternal life, and this life is
In his Son.

1 John 5:11

Lk.23,24; Mt. 27,28; Mk. 15,16; Jn. 19-21.
Lesson retold by P.Cook

But is now made manifest by the
Appearing of our Saviour Jesus Christ,
Who hath abolished death, and hath
Brought life and immortality to light
Through the gospel . . .

2 Timothy 1:10

THE BIRTH OF JESUS ON EARTH!

(A Lesson for Toddlers)

Once upon a very special time, Mary and Joseph left a city in Galilee called Nazareth to obey the law set for all the world. They went to Bethlehem, where Joseph's people lived down through the years. Mary, being great with the baby of promise by God, traveled with Joseph.

They arrived in Bethlehem very tired from the trip. (discuss with them). They went to the inn to get a room; however, the innkeeper said they were all filled up. Because there was no room for them in the inn, they went to an animal stable. There, Mary brought forth her firstborn Son and named Him Jesus. Mary and Joseph wrapped him in large clothes and laid him in a manger. (discuss what a manger is)

That same quiet night, there was much rejoicing by the angels, shepherds, and the wise men that came from afar. God had sent His only begotten Son to us. God had kept His promise that was made to mankind long, long ago. Remember, God always keeps his promises to us. He loves us one and all.

The birth of Jesus on earth; happy birthday JESUS!

Matthew 1,2; Luke 2.
Story retold by P.Cook

For unto you is born this day in the
City of David a Savior, which is
Christ the Lord.

Luke 2:11

A LOVING, CARING GOD

(For the "Tiny Tots")

God takes care
God takes care
God takes care of you and me
In the day time, the night time, in the sun, and stormy rain
God takes care of you and me.

Amen.

Unknown
(Can be repeated over and used as song lyrics)

But as it is written, eye hath not seen,
Nor ear heard, neither have entered
Into the heart of man, the things
Which God hath prepared for them
That love him.

1 Corinthians 2:9

GOD MADE THE ANIMALS ALSO

God made the first man and named him Adam. God made the first woman from the rib of a man, and she was called Eve.

Gen. 1:24,25 says:
God said, Let the earth bring forth the living creature after his kind, cattle, and creeping thing, and beast (animals) of the earth after his kind: and it was so.
God made the beast (animals) of the earth after his kind, and cattle after their kind, and everything that creepeth upon the earth after his kind: and God saw that it was good.

God created the animals. He brought them unto Adam to see what he would call them. Adam named all the animals. Let's list and spell some of the animals Adam named.

COW   C-O-W

BEAR B-E-A-R

TIGER T-I-G-E-R

MONKEY M-O-N-K-E-Y

CAT C-A-T

DOG D-O-G

SQUIRREL S-Q-U-I-R-R-E-L

FROG F-R-O-G

KANGAROO K-A-N-G-A-R-O-O

(And many more)

Many years later the rain fell upon the earth for forty days and forty nights. God told Noah, Adam's great descendant, to build an Ark (a rescue, saving boat) for the people and animals before it started to rain. The people and

The earth is the LORD'S, and the
Fullness thereof; the world, and they
That dwell therein.

Psalm 24:1

animals went into the Ark, two by two. They were safe from the flooding rain inside the Ark.

After many days, the rain stopped. The animals and people came onto the earth on dry land again. They were all so glad to be back safe on earth. God put a rainbow (discuss with the children) in the sky. God wanted to show them He would not allow it to rain, continuously, that much again.

Tell God, thank you Lord. Thank you for Jesus. Thank God that we are safe. Amen.

November, 2010
AKJV Bible

The grace of our LORD JESUS
CHRIST be with you all. AMEN.

Revelations 22:21